THE PATH OF KRIYA YOGA

Energization Exercises

*Based on the Teachings of Paramhansa Yogananda
and His Direct Disciple, Swami Kriyananda*

CRYSTAL CLARITY PUBLISHERS   Nevada City, California

© 1998, 2025 by Hansa Trust
All rights reserved. Published 1998
Reissue of the first edition 2025
Printed in the United States of America

CRYSTAL CLARITY PUBLISHERS
crystalclarity.com | clarity@crystalclarity.com
14618 Tyler Foote Rd. | Nevada City, California
800.424.1055

ISBN   978-1-56589-176-0 (print)
ISBN   978-1-56589-648-2 (e-book)
UPC   7-984994-1001-0 (audio)
ISBN   978-1-56589-304-7 (video)

Cover photograph by Barbara Bingham.
Interior layout and design by Crystal Clarity Publishers.

Ananda Church of Self-Realization was founded in 1968 by Swami Kriyananda, a direct disciple of Paramhansa Yogananda. Ananda is not affiliated with Self-Realization Fellowship.

 The *Joy Is Within You* symbol is registered by Ananda Church of Self-Realization of Nevada County, California.

Principles

Learning to Control the Subtle Energy

We are beings of energy. Matter, in fact, is merely a projection of underlying energy patterns. In this lesson you will learn a technique called the Energization Exercises, which will help you control your life-force. It would be hard to overstate the value of these exercises, which were developed by Yogananda specifically to teach us how to gain control over *prana* (subtle energy). Yogananda said that if we were stranded on a desert island and could have only one yogic technique, we should choose the Energization Exercises, because through them we would eventually discover the entire science of yoga.

As aspiring yogis, we should learn to see our bodies as the outward expression of elemental energy patterns. Our bodies, our health, our happiness, our very thoughts are determined by the level and direction of our energy. We should see our whole life as being like an image on a movie screen, simply patterns of light and dark. We have an enormously powerful tool to change ourselves, once we grasp the fact that we are merely projections of energy patterns. If we create the patterns in our lives, then it is possible to *change those patterns directly*. With that realization we have in hand the secret key to the kingdom of God, for, in reality, all that is needed to find God is to release our identification with false images of who we are.

In order to change something, it is much more effective to learn to control energy, which lies behind matter, than to try to control matter itself. Once the pattern has become frozen into its outward manifestation, it is much more difficult to change. Isn't it much easier to adjust the plans for a house than to move walls around once the house is built?

Consider this example. The introduction of computer modeling has totally transformed the way the aircraft and auto industries design and construct models of new parts. Formerly, once a new part was designed, a highly skilled craftsman had to produce a model out of wood or metal. If minor changes were needed, he had to craft the new part again and again until the new design was perfected. This process was repeated for thousands of parts. Now everything is designed with computer programs that create three-dimensional models on the screen. Parts can be matched to connecting pieces directly in the computer, where everything exists only as patterns of energy. If a physical piece is needed, it is created effortlessly by using light-sensitive plastic and computer controlled lasers. By working with energy patterns rather than physical models, the design time has been cut from years to months.

Scientists are even looking for materials, such as liquid metal, that can be formed directly into the various pieces required. Imagine an auto parts store which could produce, on demand, any part for any model of car ever made. All the necessary information would exist as energy patterns in a computer's memory.

We are not all that different from this example. We, too, exist as dynamic changing projections of underlying energy patterns. If we can learn to control our prana and change the underlying patterns sufficiently, we can work miracles for ourselves and others.

Here are just some of the benefits of being able to control and harmonize the flow of prana.

In the Body

We can have boundless energy for work, relationships, and fun. When we become tired, we can recharge the body and mind instantaneously. We can have vibrant good health, since the cells in our body would always be highly energized. If we are injured, we can heal the injuries. Does this sound impossible? It wasn't for Jesus or Yogananda or other advanced yogis. Does that mean we will never get ill? Not necessarily, but if we do get ill we can consciously direct sufficient healing energy to allow us to quickly regain our health.

In the Mind

We can easily focus the mind on the task at hand, whether work or meditation. Success is guaranteed because we are able to apply the energy needed to overcome any obstacles in our path. We would have negative moods only rarely, and if they came, we would have a way of dealing with them, since our moods and thoughts are dependent upon our level of energy. We can find it much easier to overcome unwanted attitudes and habits. We can attract to ourselves the people and circumstances that we want: The laws of magnetism are directly related to the laws of energy.

In the Soul

We can find it easy to go into deep meditation and quickly attain stillness of mind and openness of heart. Our devotion can have tremendous power and quickly attract the blessings of God and the masters. Our prayers for others and for the world can be powerful and effective. One time Yogananda and another devotee walked by Rajarshi Janakananda, Yogananda's most advanced disciple, as he was meditating in the garden. As they were passing, Yogananda cautioned the devotee to be very quiet. When they were out of hearing, he said, "You have no idea what blessings are drawn to this work simply by having one person meditate that deeply."

Results like these are possible, but they are not easy to achieve. It all starts by learning to feel and direct the flow of prana. Yogananda discovered that, through will power, we can send energy to the various parts of the body. He then made this discovery practical by devising a system of body-cell recharging called the Energization Exercises.

Techniques

These exercises are Paramhansa Yogananda's unique contribution to the science of yoga. They use a combination of concentration, will, and breath to direct the flow of energy to various body parts. This flow is sent and withdrawn by tensing and then relaxing the muscles in the area we want to recharge. Paramhansa Yogananda explained that we draw prana indirectly through the food we eat, as well as through oxygen and sunlight. These indirect sources of energy, however, are like the water you put into the battery of your car. When the battery runs down, no amount of water will make it work again. You have to recharge the battery from another source. Similarly, Yogananda explained, our bodies live only indirectly from food, but we live directly from the cosmic energy that flows into our bodies through the medulla oblongata at the base of the brain.

The lips and tongue comprise the mouth of man, because this is where we eat in a physical way, but the mouth of God is the medulla oblongata, inside the hollow point at the base of the skull. This is where we receive divine energy which truly sustains us. It is from the medulla that we will send energy to various parts of the body by tensing and relaxing the appropriate muscles.

Paramhansa Yogananda gave us the axiom, "The greater the will, the greater the flow of energy." Will power should be applied with intensity, but not grimly or with tension. It might help you to think in terms of willingness, enthusiasm, and joy. These Energization Exercises are a means of using will, with awareness of energy, to consciously draw cosmic energy into the body. As you do the movements of the exercises, try to feel the flow of energy and be conscious of that flow. Then, by use of your will power, you can direct the flow of energy to specific parts of the body. The more you become aware of using your will power to direct that energy, the more you will be able to increase the flow.

By way of illustration: Close your eyes and gaze, as in meditation, toward the spiritual eye. Concentrate your attention in the area of the medulla. Now tense your right hand and forearm, feeling that you are sending energy from the medulla to your hand and forearm. Continue tensing harder and harder until your hand is vibrating with the effort. Now relax the muscles and feel the energy in the area you have just tensed.

At first what you'll feel is just the tension inside of the muscles. Then you'll experience the flow of energy which creates the tension in those muscles. Finally, you will become aware of how you can direct that flow. It may help to visualize a flow of light. It is important, however, to try to feel the flow of energy. It is essential to concentrate as deeply as possible. Now repeat the same thing on the other side, tensing, and then relaxing, the left hand and forearm.

Key Points for Practicing the Energization Exercises

1. Concentrate on the flow of energy. Before beginning the Energization Exercises, visualize energy coming into the body through the medulla oblongata (located in the indentation at the base of the skull) and flowing through the body. Once you've learned the exercises, try to keep your eyes closed with your gaze upward toward the point between the eyebrows. This will help you to interiorize your consciousness and draw more on the superconscious. As you do the exercises, first concentrate on the center of the body part(s) that you are tensing and relaxing. Then, as you go deeper, your concentration should be *more on the flow of the energy*.

2. Use conscious will as you do the exercises. Through the use of your will, direct energy to flow into the appropriate body parts to energize the cells. Feel that, through the agency of your will, you are consciously drawing and directing the limitless stream of energy into your body. After tensing an area, completely relax and feel the results. Conscious relaxation after each exercise is very important. Tensing and relaxing not only recharges the body with energy, but even more importantly, it trains us to bring the flow of prana under our control.

3. Remember Yogananda's axiom: "The greater the will, the greater the flow of energy." This is a spiritual law. While it is better to think of will as "willingness" in order to avoid making it seem grim, you should use your will very intensely, especially during the tensing parts of the exercise. Remember: "Tense with will—relax and feel."

4. Tense gradually, and relax gradually—from low to medium to high tension. Never tense quickly, jerkily, or so hard that you cause physical discomfort. You don't want to "strip your muscle gears." Tense in a continuous wave—low, then medium, and then high with maximum tension, until the muscles vibrate. Hold the tension for up to three seconds. After tensing, relax completely—from high, to medium, to low, and finally to no tension.

5. Some of the Energization Exercises call for "double breathing." Double breathing is a short and long inhalation through the nose, and a short and long exhalation through the nose and mouth. This double breath allows you to inhale and exhale more deeply and to increase the oxygenation of the blood. To practice a "double breath," begin by inhaling strongly through the nose with a short, sharp inhalation, followed directly by a long, strong inhalation—completely filling your lungs. Then, without pause, exhale twice through the nose and mouth with a short, then a long exhalation—making the sound: "Huh, huhhhhhh" (with the breath only; do not vocalize). Feel cosmic energy flowing into the medulla oblongata with the breath.

6. It is best to practice the exercises outdoors. If you are unable to do this, make sure you do them in front of an open window or door, where fresh air can enter.

7. Practice the exercises every day at least once (and preferably twice) a day. Each exercise should be done from three to five times. Once you have learned all the exercises, it should take twelve to fifteen minutes to do them. Energization can be practiced anytime, and it is especially beneficial before meditation to release tensions, and enable you to sit still more easily and go deeper in meditation.

8. Modify if necessary. If you have back, neck, or any special physical problems or if a body part is ill or injured, modify the exercises for these body parts so as not to create discomfort. You might need to practice the exercises for these areas with low tension only, or even just mentally. It may be helpful to visualize a current of light flowing to the affected part.

9. Isolate the body part being tensed. If you cannot isolate a specific muscle or body part, put your mind there and the energy will automatically flow to that part. Later you may be able to actively locate and tense the muscles there individually.

10. Try to do all the exercises. While you are learning them, you can begin by studying and practicing a few of the exercises at a time, until you've worked up to doing them all each day. You might try practicing the first five or so exercises for a week, then adding more the next week, and so on. There are visual and audio aids that you can use to help learn the exercises more quickly—the *Ananda Energization Exercises* video, the *Energization Exercises* audio, and our *Energization Poster*.

11. Do the exercises with joy and willingness. Feel that you are giving your body a "breakfast of energy." You may want to keep this affirmation in mind as you practice: *Within me lies the energy to accomplish all that I will to do. Behind my every act is God's infinite power.*

The Energization Exercises

Do each exercise three to five times unless otherwise indicated. If an exercise alternates between both sides of the body, always start first on the left side.

Begin with this prayer:

"O, Infinite Spirit,
recharge my body with Thy Cosmic Energy,
my mind with Thy concentration,
my soul with Thy ever-new joy.
O, eternal youth of body and mind,
abide in me forever and forever."

1. Double Breathing
(with palms touching)

With your arms straight out to your sides at shoulder level, double exhale as you bring your palms together in front, bending the knees slightly. Double inhale as you straighten up and bring your arms back out to your sides, with hands as fists, tensing the entire body in an upward wave. Double exhale as you relax in a downward wave.
Do this three to five times.

2. Calf Recharging

Standing on your right foot, slowly bend your left knee, bringing your foot up behind while tensing your calf muscle. Relax momentarily, then tense the calf again as you bring your foot back down. Relax momentarily.
Do this three times with your left leg, followed by left-side Ankle Rotation (exercise #3). Then do both exercises on the right side.

3. Ankle Rotation

After the last repetition of Calf Recharging on either side, bend the knee and bring the foot up behind. Rotate the ankle in small circles, with tension around the ankle.
Rotate three times in each direction.

4. Calf-Forearm/Thigh-Upper Arm

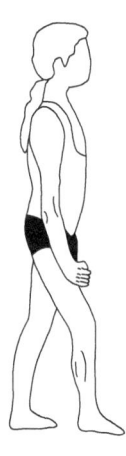

Place your left foot forward, with most of your weight on the right foot. Tense your left calf and left forearm together. Relax. Then tense your left thigh and upper arm together. Relax.

Do this sequence three times on the left, then three times on the right with your right foot forward.

Then with your weight on both legs equally, tense both calves and both forearms simultaneously. Relax, and tense both thighs and both upper arms. Relax.

Do this sequence three times, also.

5. Chest and Buttock Recharging

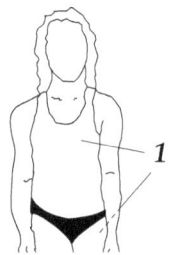

Simultaneously tense your left buttock muscles and the left side of your chest, then relax.

Repeat on the right side. Do this three times.

6. Back Recharging

Tense the muscles of your lower left back (at the waist), then relax.

Repeat on the right side. Alternate sides, tensing, and relaxing each three times.

Then tense the muscles of your middle left back, the area around the shoulder blades, then relax.

Repeat on the right side. Alternate sides, tensing, and relaxing each three times.

Then tense the muscles of your upper left back, just above the shoulder blades, then relax.

Repeat on the right side. Alternate sides, tensing, and relaxing each three times.

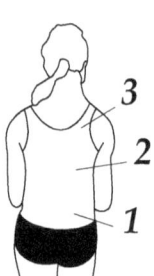

7. Shoulder Rotation

With your fingertips resting on your shoulders, rotate your arms and shoulders in large circles, with tension in the shoulders. Be sure to move your shoulders, not just your arms.

Rotate three times in one direction, then three times in the other direction.

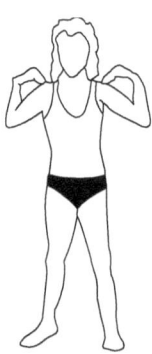

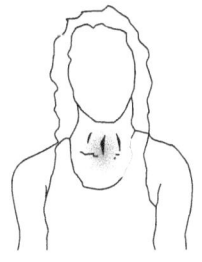

8. Throat Recharging

Tense the front of your neck and the whole throat, then relax. Do this three times. Next, tense just the left side of your neck, then relax. Tense just the right side of your neck, then relax.
Do this three times on each side.

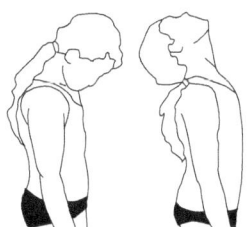

9. Neck Recharging

Gently relax your head to your chest. Then double inhale as you slowly pull it back up with tension in the back of the neck. Double exhale as you slowly relax the head back down.
Do this three times.

10. Neck Rotation

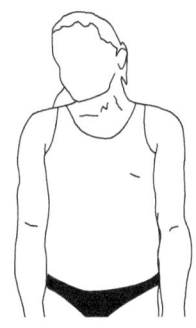

With medium tension in your neck, rotate your head and neck in small-to medium-sized circles: three times in one direction, then three times in the other direction.

Repeat the neck rotation with no tension, three times in each direction.

Whether with or without tension, the circles should be the same size. Rotate from the base of the neck, not from the top of the neck.

Caution: For neck safety, don't "grind" the neck, or bend it backward sharply, or let the head flop around. If your neck is vulnerable, keep the circles small; you can also lift your shoulders for extra neck support.

11. Spinal Recharging
(lower back adjustment)

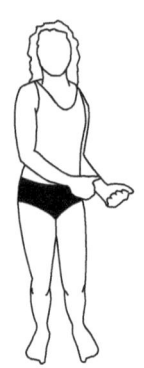

Stand with your feet apart, legs straight. Twist your upper body, shoulders, and arms in one direction while you twist your hips and lower body slightly in the opposite direction (a quick yet smooth motion). Your feet should remain stationary, your elbows slightly bent, your fists positioned about hip level, and head pointed forward.

Alternate twisting to the left and right. Twist each way three or more times.

12. Spinal Rotation

Stand with your feet apart and your hands at your waist. Bend forward at the hips and arch your back slightly. With your hips stationary, and keeping the arch in your back with tension, rotate your trunk in small circles.

Three times in one direction, then repeat three in the other, relaxing momentarily in between.

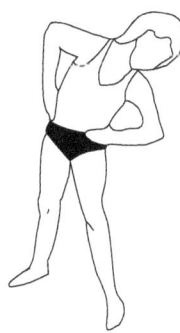

13. Spinal Stretching
(from side to side)

Stand with your feet apart and hands on your hips at your waist. Maintain tension along the spine as you bend your upper body to the left, then to the right. Keep your lower body stationary, including your hips, and keep your head in line with the spine. Move only from the waist upward.
Do this three times.

14. Spinal Adjustment

Place your knuckles or thumbs on the muscles on each side of the base of the spine. Bend slightly forward, then press your hands firmly into your back and arch your spine, drawing your head and upper body slightly up and back.

Repeat, working up the spine as high as you can go.
Caution: Do not snap your back in a violent motion. Rather feel the steady pressure of the fists on the back pushing you forward.

15. Upper Spinal Twisting
(with arms from side to side)

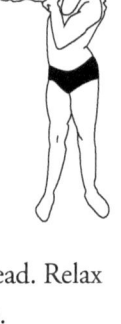

Stand with your feet apart, arms straight out in front of you at shoulder height, with the fists facing each other. Keeping your hips stationary, twist your upper body and arms from side to side. Hold tension in your arms as you twist; release it at the end of your twist. Keep your leading arm straight and allow the trailing arm to bend at the elbow. Follow your hands with your eyes and head. Relax forward to the initial position, then repeat to the other side.
Do this three times in each direction.

16. Skull Tapping / Memory Exercise

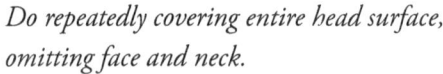

Briskly rap your skull and forehead all over with your knuckles to stimulate the energy in the brain. Visualize all your brain cells being awakened with cosmic energy.
Do repeatedly covering entire head surface, omitting face and neck.

17. Scalp Massage

Press your fingertips firmly on your head, and rotate small areas of your scalp in circles. Move the scalp over the skull; don't merely rub the head. Push down with your fingers hard enough to feel the skin moving. Then move the fingers on the head to another position.
Continue until you've massaged the entire scalp.

18. Medulla Massage

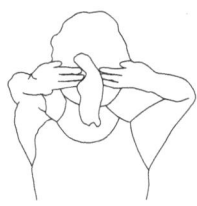

With the first three fingers of each hand, massage the medulla (the depression just below the base of the skull) in small circles: three times in one direction, then three times the other direction. Then double inhale as you arch your head slowly back against the pressure of your fingers, tensing your neck. Double exhale as you relax and gently press your head forward with the fingers, bringing your chin to your chest.

Do this sequence three times.

19. Biceps Recharging

Clasp your hands above your head, or on your head. Tense and relax your left biceps muscles — the muscles in your left upper arm. Then tense and relax your right biceps.

Alternate doing each side three times. Keep the hands relaxed.

20. Twenty-Part Body Recharging

Phase 1—Tense the entire body simultaneously. With a double inhalation, gradually tense all body muscles simultaneously (low-medium-high), vibrate the whole body strongly, and relax gradually with a double exhalation.

Phase 2—Tense and Relax the 20 body parts individually. Gradually tense and relax each of the twenty body parts individually, alternating from left to right: feet, calves, thighs, buttocks, lower and upper abdominal muscles, forearms, upper arms, chest muscles, neck (left side, right side, front and back).

Phase 3—Tense the 20 body parts, holding the tension. Repeat the exercise, this time maintaining the tension at a medium level in each part, as you slowly inhale. When the entire body is tense, vibrate it briefly and strongly, and then …

Phase 4—Relax each muscle individually in the reverse order as you slowly exhale. Begin the relaxation phase by bringing the chin to the chest and thus relaxing all four parts of the neck.

Phase 5—With the chin still on the chest, double inhale and gradually tense, and vibrate the whole body, and then gradually relax, with a double exhalation.

The Energization Exercises

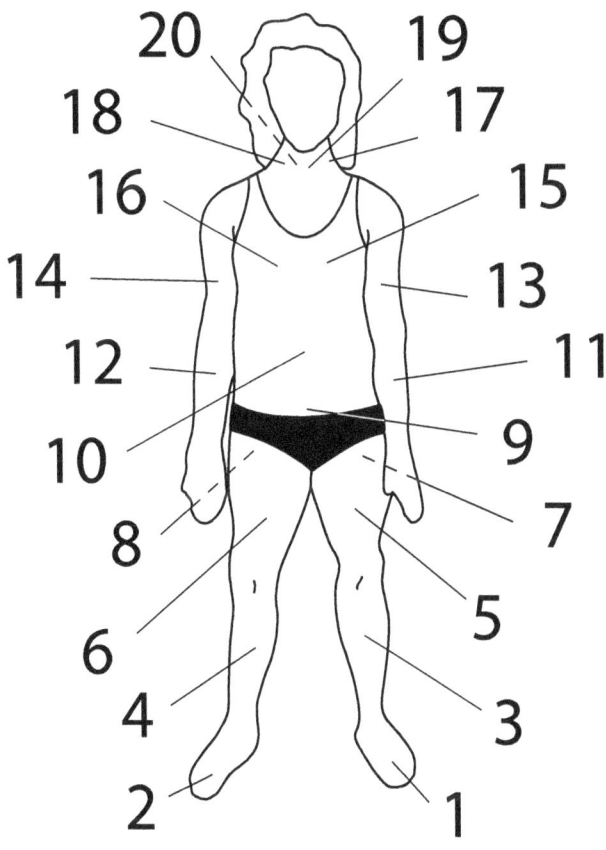

21. Lifting Weights in Front

Stand with your arms at your sides and your hands in fists, palms facing each other. Bend at the elbows and bring the hands up, tensing as though lifting heavy weights. Relax momentarily. Then push the hands back down, with tension. Relax momentarily, then repeat.

Do this three times.

Optional: Double inhale as you lift the hands, double exhale as you press them down.

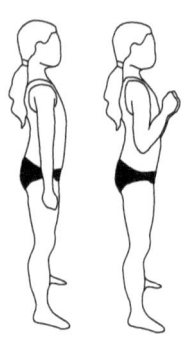

22. Double Breathing
    (with elbows touching)

With your arms out at your sides, bent 90 degrees at the elbows, double exhale and bring your elbows and fists together in front, facing each other. As in exercise #1, double inhale and tense in a wave, then double exhale and relax in a wave. Here, keep your hands in fists, elbows bent, and upper arms horizontal throughout.

Do this three to five times.

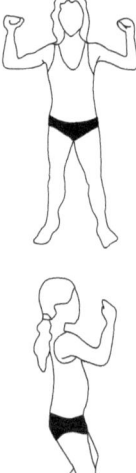

23. Pulling Weights from the Side

Extend your arms straight out to your sides at shoulder level. Make fists, palms facing up. With tension in the arms, draw the fists toward the head, then relax momentarily. Press the fists away from your head with tension, then relax momentarily. *Do this three times.*

Optional: Double inhale as you bring the arms in, double exhale as you extend them out.

24. Arm Rotation
(in small circles)

Stand with your arms extended straight out to your sides at shoulder level and your hands in fists, palms facing up. Rotate your arms several times in small circles with increasing tension.

Relax briefly, then repeat in the opposite direction.

25. Pulling Weights from the Front

Begin with your fists at your forehead, palms facing forward. With tension in the arms as though pushing weights, straighten your arms out in front, then relax. Bring your hands back to your forehead as if pulling weights in, then relax.
Do this three times in each direction.
Optional: Double inhale as you bring the arms in, double exhale as you extend them out.

26. Finger Recharging

Beginning with your arms at your sides, open and close your hands several times with tension in your hands and fingers: quickly squeeze your hands into fists, then "burst" open your fists. Repeat with your arms straight out to your sides at shoulder height, then straight out in front, and finally extended overhead.

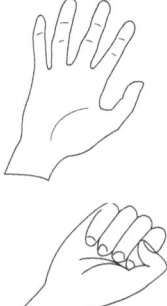

27. Four-Part Arm Recharging

Bring your fists to chest level. Tense your arms and in a continuous motion push the fists out to the side. Then pull them back to the chest and push the arms out to the front. Then return them to the chest and sweep them up above your head, rising up on your toes as you reach full extension. End by coming down off your toes and relaxing the arms, first to your chest and then lowering your hands to your sides. The arms should be tensed throughout these movements, but relaxed momentarily at the points where they are fully extended and when the fists touch the chest. The breathing is as follows: Inhale as you extend the arms from the chest outward to the sides and back to the chest. Exhale with the movement pushing forward and coming back to the chest. Double inhale as you extend the arms above your head. Finally, double exhale as you relax them down to the waist.

Repeat three times.

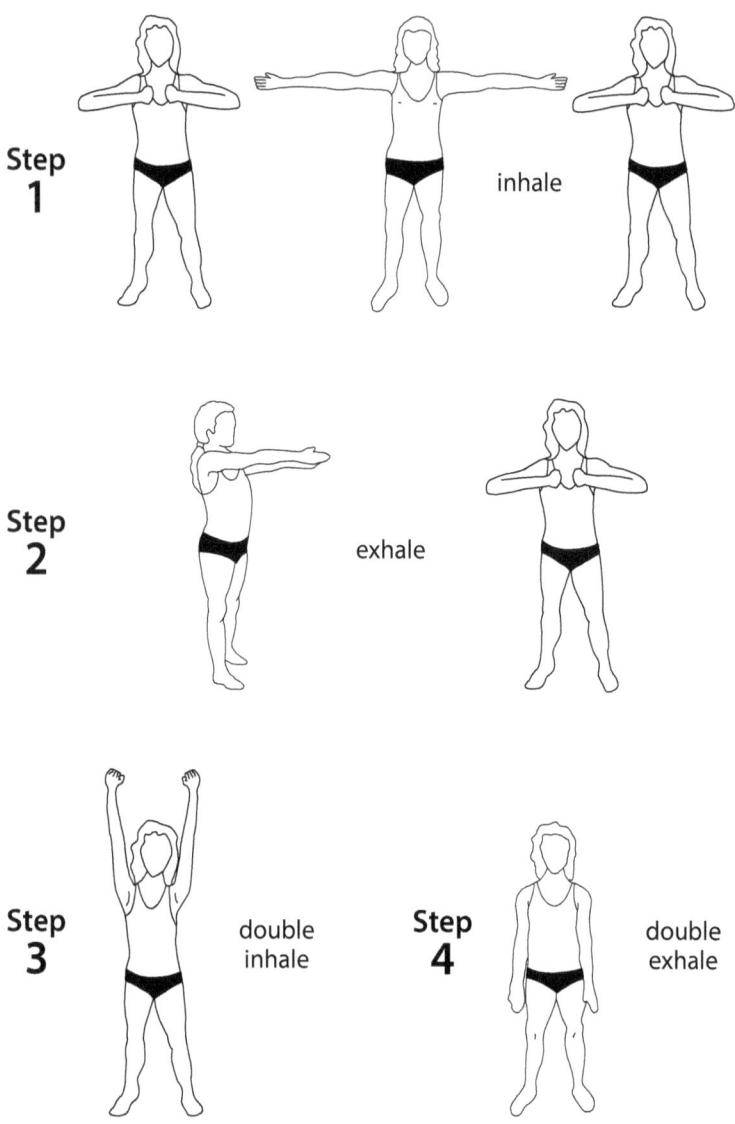

28. Single Arm Recharging

Stand with both arms down to your sides. Double inhale as you tense your straightened left arm, with hand in a fist, and lift it forward and up over your head (as if you are lifting a weight). Double exhale as you relax the arm back down to your side. Repeat with the right arm.

Alternate doing both sides three times.

Optional: You can rise up onto your toes as you do this.

29. Stretching Side to Side

Stand with both arms down at your sides, and your feet apart. Double inhale as you tense your left arm, with hand in a fist, out to the side and up near your head (again, as if you are lifting a weight), then continue its swing as you bend your upper body at the waist to your right. Don't let your head drop over to the side; keep it up against the arm. Double exhale as you relax down.

Repeat with the right arm, bending your body to the left. Alternate doing each side three times.

30. Walking in Place

Walk in place with an exaggerated marching step, lifting your knees high (until your thighs are parallel to the floor) and swinging the opposite arm as you march. Try to keep your concentration on the flow of energy; remember that the movement in this exercise is secondary to becoming aware of the energy in the different body parts and sending that energy to those parts that you are moving.

Repeat 25–50 times.

31. Running in Place

Run vigorously in place with a bouncing step, lifting your knees and thighs up high, and if possible, bringing your heels up to strike your buttocks. Do not move the arms; hold your bent elbows steady throughout the exercise.

Repeat 25–50 times.

32. Fencing

Start with both fists at your chest. Double exhale as you step your left foot forward and thrust your right arm forward, tensing the entire right side of your body (as though closing a heavy door). Don't lean forward as you thrust but stay centered over the middle of your body. Keep the back heel on the floor as you step forward. Double inhale as you step back and relax into the initial position. Repeat to the other side.

Do each side three times, alternating. (Make sure you are extending the opposite arm and leg.)

33. Arm Rotation
(in large circles)

Double inhale as you swing both of your tensed arms, with hands in fists, behind you and up overhead in large circles. Double exhale as you relax them forward and down. Do this three times. Then reverse direction, double inhaling as you swing your tensed arms forward and up, double exhaling as you relax them behind and down.

Do this three times.

34. Abdominal Recharging

Exhale fully and bend over slightly, resting the heels of your hands on the tops of your thighs. Without inhaling, draw your abdomen strongly toward your spine. Hold. When needed, relax, straighten up and inhale. Repeat: This time draw the abdomen in and push it out, strongly and rhythmically, several times, with breath held out. Repeat once more, or as an alternative, rotate and churn the abdominal muscles. (This is a very good exercise for stimulating the digestion and the internal organs.)

35. Double Breathing
(with palms touching)
Repeat exercise number one.

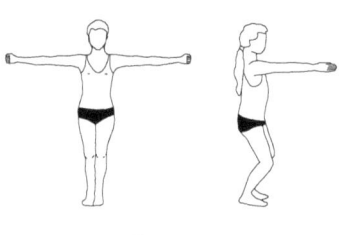

36. Calf Recharging
Repeat exercise number two.

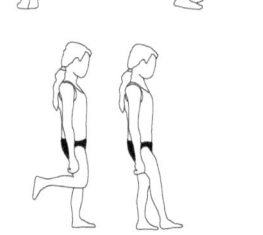

37. Ankle Rotation
Repeat exercise number three.

38. Hip Recharging

Standing on your right foot, rotate your straightened left leg in large circles (with your relaxed left foot just clearing the floor). Then rotate it in the opposite direction. Switch to the opposite leg and repeat. Focus on sending energy to your hip, which this exercise specifically helps.
Rotate each leg three times in each direction.

39. Double Breathing
(without tension)

With elbows bent and hands in a relaxed fist position facing forward, draw your hands towards your upper chest and shoulder area. Close your eyes and focus your attention at the point between the eyebrows. Softly double exhale as you extend your arms and hands in front, and hold them there. Enjoy the pause between breaths. Softly double inhale as you bring your hands back to your chest. Enjoy that pause as well. Do not tense your arms during this exercise. Feel relaxed, peaceful, and energized.
Repeat 6–10 times.

Quotes on Energization
From the *Yogoda Lessons*
by Paramhansa Yogananda
Copyright 1924

"Yogoda [Energization] teaches how to surround each body cell with a ring of super-charged electrical vital energy and thus keep free from decay of bacterial invasion. It keeps not only the muscles, but all the tissues of the body, bones, marrow, brain, and cells in perfect health."

"Yogoda brings about the growth of all the cells and tissues. It teaches how to recharge the body battery with fresh life current by increasing the will power. It gives specific methods to strengthen and recharge the muscles—not only collectively, but individually—with vital force. It establishes harmony between the working of the voluntary muscles and the involuntary processes. And this harmony gives wonderful health and strength."

"Yogoda causes the resurrection of dying tissue cells and worn out facilities and the formation of billions of new cells and fresh facilities, all through the right exercise of will. Through it all the various tissues—bony, muscular, connective, nerve, etc.—are proportionately formed and the mind is strengthened. The circulation, respiration, digestion, and all other involuntary processes of the body are harmonized and invigorated; the mind is clarified."

"Yogoda teaches the art of consciously sending the curative life energy to any diseased body part. By its aid the general vitality of the body is markedly raised, resulting in a wonderful development of tissue, strength, and unexpected nerve vigor, thereby insuring greater longevity. Memory and brain power are also increased through greater blood supply."

Spiritual Roots

The *The Path of Kriya Yoga* is based on the teachings of Paramhansa Yogananda, author of the spiritual classic *Autobiography of a Yogi*. Yogananda was the first great Indian master of yoga to make his home in the West. By sharing with countless Americans the life-transforming techniques of yoga and meditation, he opened the door to their own direct experience of spiritual realities.

• • • • •

"As a bright light shining in the midst of darkness, so was Yogananda's presence in this world. Such a great soul comes on earth only rarely, when there is a real need among men."

—The Shankaracharya of Kanchipuram

PARAMHANSA YOGANANDA, born in 1893, was the first yoga master of India to take up permanent residence in the West. Yogananda arrived in America in 1920, and proceeded to travel throughout the country on what he called his "spiritual campaigns." Hundreds of thousands filled the largest halls in major cities to see the yoga master from India. Yogananda continued to lecture and write up to his passing in 1952.

Yogananda's initial impact on Western culture was truly impressive. But his lasting spiritual legacy has been even greater. His *Autobiography of a Yogi*, first published in 1946, helped launch a spiritual revolution in the West. Translated into more than a dozen languages, it remains a best-selling spiritual classic to this day.

Before embarking on his mission, Yogananda received this admonition from his teacher, Swami Sri Yukteswar: "The West is high in material attainments but lacking in spiritual understanding. It is God's will that you play a role in teaching mankind the value of balancing the material with an inner, spiritual life."

In addition to *Autobiography of a Yogi*, Yogananda's spiritual legacy includes music, poetry, and extensive commentaries on the Bhagavad Gita, the *Rubaiyat* of Omar Khayyam, and the Christian Bible, showing the principles of Self-realization as the unifying truth underlying all true religions. Through his teachings and his Kriya Yoga path millions of people around the world have found a new way to connect personally with God.

His mission, however, was far broader than all this. It was to help usher the whole world into Dwapara Yuga, the new Age of Energy in which we live. "Someday," Swami Kriyananda wrote, "I believe he will be seen as the *avatar* of Dwapara Yuga: the way shower for a new age."

"Swami Kriyananda is a man of wisdom and compassion in action, truly one of the leading lights in the spiritual world today."

—Lama Surya Das, Dzogchen Center, author of
Awakening The Buddha Within

SWAMI KRIYANANDA prolific author, accomplished composer, playwright, and artist, and a world-renowned spiritual teacher, Swami Kriyananda (1926–2013) referred to himself simply as "a humble disciple" of the great God-realized master, Paramhansa Yogananda. He met his guru at the age of twenty-two, and served him during the last four years of the Master's life. He dedicated the rest of his life to sharing Yogananda's teachings throughout the world.

Kriyananda was born in Romania of American parents, and educated in Europe, England, and the United States. Philosophically and artistically inclined from youth, he soon came to question life's meaning and society's values. During a period of intense inward reflection, he discovered Yogananda's *Autobiography of a Yogi*, and immediately traveled three thousand miles from New York to California to meet the Master, who accepted him as a monastic disciple. Yogananda appointed him as the head of the monastery, authorized him to teach and give Kriya Initiation in his name, and entrusted him with the missions of writing and developing what he called "world brotherhood colonies."

Kriyananda founded the first such community, Ananda Village, in the Sierra Nevada foothills of Northern California in 1968. Ananda is recognized as one of the most successful interntional communities in the world today. It has served as a model for other such communities that he founded subsequently in the United States, Europe, and India.

The Path of Kriya Yoga

Kriya Yoga is a meditation technique that quickly accelerates one's spiritual growth. It was first made widely known by Paramhansa Yogananda in his *Autobiography of a Yogi*. According to Yogananda, Kriya is the most effective technique available to mankind today for reaching the goal of Yoga: union with the Divine.

At Ananda we teach Kriya Yoga just as Yogananda taught it. Yogananda taught Kriya Yoga as part of a comprehensive spiritual path that includes three other techniques (Energization Exercises, *Hong-Sau*, AUM Meditation), along with discipleship to the Kriya line of Gurus. The actual Kriya technique is given through initiation, after establishing a regular daily practice of the first three techniques. This process takes about a year or more, depending on the student.

The Path of Kriya courses can be done either in-person or online. If you live near one of our Ananda Centers, we encourage you to take advantage of the opportunity to learn the techniques face-to-face. For those who are not near an Ananda Center, our online classes provide an equally effective way to learn.

Whether you choose to study in-person or online (or a combination thereof), you will receive personalized spiritual support, access to valuable resources, and ample opportunities to ask questions of our experienced meditation teachers.

The Path of Kriya Yoga Online Courses

Step 1 *Ananda Course in Meditation*

This 10-week course, based on *Lessons in Meditation* by Nayaswami Jyotish, introduces you to transformative techniques from the path of Kriya Yoga, including the *Hong-Sau* method of concentration and the *Energization Exercises*. You'll learn how to sit comfortably for meditation, quiet the restless mind, and carry the peace and joy of your practice into daily life. With guidance and support, this course will help you establish a steady and fulfilling meditation routine.

Step 2 *Living the Principles of Self-Realization*

This 10-week course, based on *The Art and Science of Raja Yoga* by Swami Kriyananda, provides a comprehensive exploration of Raja Yoga and Patanjali's eight-limbed path. With meditation as its core practice, the course offers lessons and practical tools to help spiritualize all aspects of life. Its primary focus is to prepare participants for Kriya Yoga initiation, offering a deeper understanding of this transformative spiritual path.

Step 3 *Course on Discipleship*

This 10-week course, based on *A Handbook on Discipleship* by Swami Kriyananda, offers profound insights into the meaning of discipleship and the practice of the Guru-Disciple relationship. Through inspiring stories and personal experiences, the course helps prepare students for initiation into discipleship—either at home or in person—to Yogananda and the lineage of Masters of Self-Realization, for those who feel ready to embrace this deeper commitment.

Step 4 *Preparation for Kriya Yoga*

This 14-week course provides instruction in the AUM technique of meditation and offers further preparation for Kriya Yoga initiation. Available by permission from the Ananda Kriya Sangha after completing the first three steps of the Path of Kriya, the course builds on previous teachings while deepening your practice. Participants receive personalized, one-on-one guidance and support from instructors, ensuring a meaningful and transformative experience.

Kriya Yoga Initiation

After completion of the Path of Kriya Yoga training, having established a regular daily spiritual practice using the main techniques as taught on this path, and approved by Ananda Kriya Sangha, Kriya is received through the Kriya initiation ceremony.

Ananda Kriya Sangha contact information

kriyayoga@ananda.org

www.ananda.org/kriya-yoga

Ananda Kriya Sangha
14618 Tyler Foote Road
Nevada City, CA 95959

Resources

CRYSTAL CLARITY PUBLISHERS

If you enjoyed this title, Crystal Clarity Publishers invites you to deepen If you enjoyed this title, Crystal Clarity Publishers invites you to deepen your spiritual life through many additional resources based on the teachings of Paramhansa Yogananda. We offer books, e-books, audiobooks, yoga and meditation videos, and a wide variety of inspirational and relaxation music composed by Swami Kriyananda.

See a listing of books below, visit our secure website for a complete online catalog, or place an order for our products

crystalclarity.com
800.424.1055 | clarity@crystalclarity.com
14618 Tyler Foote Road | Nevada City, CA 95959

ANANDA WORLDWIDE

Crystal Clarity Publishers is the publishing house of Ananda, a worldwide spiritual movement founded by Swami Kriyananda, a direct disciple of Paramhansa Yogananda. Ananda offers resources and support for your spiritual journey through meditation instruction, webinars, online virtual community, email, and chat.

Ananda has more than 150 centers and meditation groups in over 45 countries, offering group guided meditations, classes and teacher training in meditation and yoga, and many other resources.

In addition, Ananda has developed eight residential communities in the US, Europe, and India. Spiritual communities are places where people live together in a spirit of cooperation and friendship, dedicated to a common goal. Spirituality is practiced in all areas of daily life: at school, at work, or in the home. Many Ananda communities offer internships during which one can stay and experience spiritual community firsthand.

For more information about Ananda communities or meditation groups near you, please visit ananda.org or call 530.478.7560.

THE EXPANDING LIGHT RETREAT

The Expanding Light is the largest retreat center in the world to share exclusively the teachings of Paramhansa Yogananda. Situated in the Ananda Village community near Nevada City, California, the center offers the opportunity to experience spiritual life in a contemporary ashram setting. The varied, year-round schedule of classes and programs on yoga, meditation, and spiritual practice includes Karma Yoga, personal retreat, spiritual travel, and online learning. Large groups are welcome.

The Ananda School of Yoga & Meditation offers certified yoga, spiritual counselor, and meditation teacher trainings.

The teaching staff has years of experience practicing Kriya Yoga meditation and all aspects of Paramhansa Yogananda's teachings. You may come for a relaxed personal renewal, participating in ongoing activities as much or as little as you wish. The serene mountain setting, supportive staff, and delicious vegetarian meals provide an ideal environment for a truly meaningful stay, be it a brief respite or an extended spiritual vacation.

For more information, please visit expandinglight.org or call 800.346.5350.

ANANDA MEDITATION RETREAT

Set amidst seventy-two acres of beautiful meditation gardens and wild forest in Northern California's Sierra foothills, the Ananda Meditation Retreat is an ideal setting for a rejuvenating, inner experience.

The Meditation Retreat has been a place of deep meditation and sincere devotion for over fifty years. Long before that, the Native American Maidu tribe held this to be sacred land. The beauty and presence of the Divine are tangibly felt by all who visit here.

Studies show that being in nature and using techniques such as forest bathing can significantly reduce stress and blood pressure while strengthening your immune system, concentration, and level of happiness. The Meditation Retreat is the perfect place for quiet immersion in nature.

Plan a personal retreat, enjoy one of the guided retreats, or choose from a variety of programs led by the caring and joyful staff.

For more information or to make your reservation, please visit meditationretreat.org, email meditationretreat@ananda.org, or call 530.478.7557.

Energization Exercises Practice Aids

Video: On track one, Gyandev McCord presents the exercises with detailed instruction. On track two, Melody Hansen demonstrates slower practice. On track three, a medium practice session is led by Badri Matlock. On track four, Gyandev leads a faster session. And on track five is a special practice session with Swami Kriyananda.

Wall poster: with the complete descriptions and illustrations.

Guided Audio: for those that need an audio reminder on how to do these exercises. Track one has a detailed description of the exercises. Track two is in a "call-out" style of each exercise name to help you through the complete set.

www.ingramcontent.com/pod-product-compliance
Lightning Source LLC
Chambersburg PA
CBHW040323050426
42453CB00018B/2445